WORTH MORE THAN DIAMONDS

WORTH MORE THAN DIAMONDS

Discover Your Priceless Value to God. You are Made to Shine!

By:

Christina Leeman, MPH, CHES

WORTH MORE THAN DIAMONDS

WORTH MORE THAN DIAMONDS
Discover Your Priceless Value to God. You are Made to Shine!

Copyright © 2019 by Christina Leeman

All rights reserved. No part of this book may be reproduced, scanned, or distributed in any printed or electronic form without permission.
First Edition: October 2019
Printed in the United States of America

Published by She Who Honors publications

Cover and interior design by Christina Leeman of She Who Honors

www.SheWhoHonors.com

www.WorthMTDiamonds.com

Scripture taken from the International Children's Bible®. Copyright © 1986, 1988, 1999 by Thomas Nelson. Used by permission. All rights reserved.

ISBN: 978-0-578-57037-2

To Alajane', Noelle, Jalise, the twins and all of God's beautiful girls, you are loved very much by an awesome God.

Intro

Hello! I'm so glad you are reading this booklet! You are not alone with whatever you are dealing with. There are adults who really care about you. God loves you!

A long time ago when I was in middle school, I had a rough time. I was quiet, a little overweight, cried easily, sensitive and didn't have many friends.

However, I knew about God and his Son Jesus. Jesus sacrificed His life for me and everyone else (even the bully's). He died so I could be cleaned from my sins and be with God again!

Knowing about God's love helped me. Being in a loving family assisted me, too. But at that age it was still hard for me to be happy at times because of all the changes in my brain.

During the teen years the pre – frontal cortex of the brain changes and matures into an adult brain. The hormones are working in overdrive, too.

INTRODUCTION

The teen years can be hard, no lie. But you will get through it.

I believed in God and myself to get through the hard middle and high school years. I went to college graduated, got a job, then met a man who became my husband. We became parents. I went back to school to get my masters.

Trusting, believing, and obeying God throughout my life journey meant that even though I experienced hard times, I survived.

I wrote this book for you to know and believe a few truths about your value and God's love for you.

You will experience negative words by the culture, your friends, peers, parents, family, teachers, coaches, vines, memes and texts. That's a fact! But know this: you have beauty, value, love and purpose in God's eye, and that is all that matters!

Stand strong in your faith and hope in Jesus.

"I leave you peace. My peace I give you. I do

not give it to you as the world does. So don't let your hearts be troubled. Don't be afraid." John 14: 27

Grab your Bible so you can look up the verses in the booklet. Here we go!

Christina

Christina@shewhohonors.com

WWW.WorthMTDiamonds.com

YOU ARE BRILLIANT, BEAUTIFUL, BLESSED AND BELOVED!

CONTENTS

I Am Beautiful	1
God Loves Me	9
I Am Worth More Than Diamonds	16
I Am God's Girl	21
I Am in Charge of Me	27
Special Prayer for You	35
Good News	38

WORTH MORE THAN DIAMONDS

"No, your beauty should come from within you—the beauty of a gentle and quiet spirit. This beauty will never disappear, and it is worth very much to God." 1 Peter 3: 4

God made girls and women as creatures of beauty. Your beauty is more than looks. Beauty is your attitude, character and personality. Beauty is found on the inside.

A diamond is formed deep in the earth from extreme pressure and heat. After it's cut and polished its beauty shines!

I AM BEAUTIFUL

I'm sure you know of a celebrity or classmate who looks pretty but when their actions are mean it causes them to look ugly!

You know the Cinderella story? Cinderella is a sweet young lady who loves her dad, animals, and life. Beautiful on the inside and outside, kind Cinderella never complained.

The wicked stepsisters in the story treat Cinderella with hurtful actions and mean attitudes. Although they too were pretty, their rude character made them ugly.

There is nothing wrong with wanting to look pretty, getting your hair and nails done or wearing trendy clothes. I like those, too!

It's when we focus on the outward appearance as being more important than what's inside of us, this can cause us pain in our lives.

Work on your insides first! Do you think positive? Do you behave in a positive manner?

Don't worry if sometimes you aren't feeling or acting positive. I know some days will be rough. Send a little prayer out to God and ask Him to help you be kind, patient, nice, etc.

When you accept Jesus as your Lord and Savior, the Holy Spirit dwells in you. The Holy Spirit will help you have a positive attitude by dressing your insides with the fruit of the Spirit.

Fruit of the Spirit

Just like fruit is sweet and good, the fruit of the Spirit are sweet and good for you (and for others)!

What is your favorite fruit? My favorite fruit is a nectarine. They are sweet, crunchy and yummy. I like to call fruit "nature's dessert"

Turn to the book of Galatians, chapter 5, verses 22-23; these verses tell of the fruit of the Holy Spirit.

"But the Spirit gives love, joy, peace, patience, kindness, goodness, faithfulness, gentleness, self-control. There is no law that says these things are wrong." Galatians 5: 22-23

These fruits of the Spirit are to help you and others experience God's love.

Precious in God's Eyes

God doesn't make junk. You are His beautiful poem. A work of art! You are unique. One of a kind. There is no one like you and there will never be. You are special and you have a special place in this world.

WORTH MORE THAN DIAMONDS

Diamonds are one of the world's most precious gems. You are one of God's most precious gems!

Go to the book of Psalms in your Bible and find chapter 139 verses 13-16.

"You made my whole being. You formed me in my mother's body. I praise you because you made me in an amazing way. What you have done is wonderful. I know this very well. You saw my bones being formed as I took shape in my mother's body. When I was put together there, you saw my body as it was formed. All the days planned for me were written in your book before I was one day old." Psalms 139: 13-16

Aren't those verses awesome?!

It's not what the world says about you; it's what God says that really matters!

Take action:

♡ Write down all the things you love about yourself.

♡ Write down all the things you are thankful for.

♡ Good characteristics are honesty, patience, kindness, loving, gentleness and helpfulness. Write down your good character traits.

♡ Write down the names of adults you know who have good character. How do you feel about them? How do they make you feel?

♡ Remember you are beautiful and precious in His sight!!

I AM BEAUTIFUL

Space for your thoughts:

GOD LOVES ME!

"For God loved the world so much that he gave his only Son. God gave his Son so that whoever believes in him may not be lost, but have eternal life. John 3:16

God loves you and me so much that He sacrificed his son, Jesus so we can be with Him forever! You are worth dying for!

Do you have a favorite superhero? I like Wonder Woman. She is beautiful, strong, kind and fast. She saves countless people from evil villains.

Jesus is like a superhero. He saves us from evil and the wrong we do. He saves us from ourselves! He also gives us power to fight against evil.

Your life may not be as action - packed as a superhero movie, but you do have power. Power in your choices!

Jesus saves us because of His great love for us. His love is power.

He is so powerful He rose from the dead three days later! He is alive and back again with His father God. Cheering and praying for you.

A sacrifice is a selfless act of love. God loves you with an everlasting love.

Go to the book of Romans chapter 8 and verses 38-39 in your Bible:

"Yes, I am sure that nothing can separate us from the love God has for us. Not death, not life, not angels, not ruling spirits, nothing now, nothing in the future, no powers, nothing above us, nothing below us, or anything else in the whole world will ever be able to separate us from the love of God that is in Christ Jesus our Lord." Romans 8: 38-39

How many pieces of hair do you have on your head? That's a hard question to answer, but God knows the answer! God loves and knows every detail about you.

Go to the book of Luke chapter 12 and verses 6-7:

"When five sparrows are sold, they cost only two pennies. But God does not forget any of them. Yes, God even knows how many hairs you have on your head. Don't be afraid. You are worth much more than many sparrows." Luke 12: 6-7

GOD LOVES ME

A sparrow is a little bird. They are very social with each other. Sparrows are common in the USA.

Just as God loves you, he wants you to love yourself and others. Respect yourself and others, pray for one another.

Go to John chapter 13 verses 34-35:

"I give you a new command: Love each other. You must love each other as I have loved you. All people will know that you are my followers if you love each other." John 13: 34-35

Take action:

⭐ Write this down: "I am important. I matter to God. God loves me!" Put it on your mirror and look at it every day.

⭐ What is special to you?

⭐ God loves you with an everlasting love. Believe it. Receive it.

⭐ Love one another.

Space for your thoughts:

_____

_____

_____

_____

_____

_____

_____

WORTH MORE THAN DIAMONDS

WORTH MORE THAN DIAMONDS

The Hope Diamond is a large blue diamond. It was owned by many different people. Some of its owners were French Kings, British nobility and jewelers - Piere Cartier was one.

Mrs. Evalyn Walsh McLean from Washington, D.C. bought the Hope diamond mounted on a headpiece from Carteir and had it until 1947.

Last Harry Winston bought Mrs. McLean's entire jewelry collection - including the Hope diamond

WORTH MORE THAN DIAMONDS

Harry Winston is a gemologist. He opened his House of Harry Winston in 1932 in New York city. He was known as the "king of Diamonds." Mr. Winston was a well known jewelry designer.

Harry Winston donated the Hope diamond to the Smithsonian Institution in Washington, DC.

The Hope diamond is set in a pendant with sixteen diamonds circling it. The necklace part is made of smaller white diamonds. There is a total of forty - five white diamonds in the necklace! The Hope Diamond is valued at 350 million dollars!

Diamonds are the hardest material on earth. They are 58x harder than anything else!

The Hope Diamond is in the Smithsonian museum in Washington, D.C. for everyone to see.

You are worth more than 350 million dollars. You are priceless to God. You are more important than the Hope Diamond - God thinks you are worth dying for!

WORTH MORE THAN DIAMONDS

Value yourself and others because we are made in God's image. You are important and matter deeply to God. Everyone is special to God.

Take action:

- Know your worth. Write down "I am worth it!"
- Who is important to you?
- What is important to you?

Space for your thoughts:

_____

_____

_____

_____

_____

_____

_____

_____

WORTH MORE THAN DIAMONDS

I AM GOD'S GIRL!

"So God created human beings in his image. In the image of God he created them. He created them male and female." Genesis 1: 27

You are one of God's awesome creations. You were created in his image. You have the Spirit of God in you.

Diamonds are very unique. It is the only gem made of one element: 99.5% carbon!

When you accept and believe in God's son Jesus Christ as your Lord and Savior you become adopted into God's family! You inherit the kingdom of God and become a princess!

Go to the book of Galatians chapter 4 and verse 4:

"But when the right time came, God sent his Son. His Son was born of a woman and lived under the law. God did this so that he could buy freedom for those who were under the law. His purpose was to make us his children." Galatians 4: 4-5

Isn't that awesome! You and I are royalty. Having Jesus Christ as our Lord and Savior and trusting and obeying Him and the Bible makes your life much better.

Jesus came so we can enjoy life the way God created us to. He does so much for those who love Him.

Turn to the book of Romans chapter 8 verse 28:

"We know that in everything God works for the good of those who love him. They are the people God called, because that was his plan." Romans 8: 28

So, who are you?

You are God's girl.

I Am God's Girl!

I AM GOD'S GIRL
Your identity

During your teen years is when you really start to think about who you are: identity. Your identity is made up of all that you are. These are strengths and characteristics that a person is born with.

Some of my strengths are good communicator, creative, visionary and achiever. Can you think of strengths that you have?

Some of my identity traits are being a woman, a cook and a writer. However, some identities can change. Like being someone's girlfriend; after a breakup girlfriend is no longer an identity. And when this identity changes your world shouldn't come crashing down.

Remember the first thing; you are a child of God. That is a firm identity that will never change.

Take action:

- Read your Bible daily. Stay in God's word.
- Write down some of your strengths.
- Why is your identity in God a strong identity?
- Remember you are a Princess!

Space for your thoughts:

_____

_____

_____

_____

_____

_____

_____

I AM GOD'S GIRL

I AM IN CHARGE OF ME

"Listen, my child, and be wise. Keep your mind on what is right." Proverbs 23:19

God created you to think, feel and choose. You are able to think before you say something. You can choose what outfit you will wear to church. You can feel happiness when eating your favorite candy.

Your brain is different than your mind. Don't worry I'm not going to get too scientific! You are in control of what you think (your mind) and much of what you do.

As you get older you will realize this. You are

in charge of you. You are in charge of your actions, what you say and what you do.

Becoming a teen and into adult years, the phrase "She made me do it" won't cut it. This doesn't work because you can think before you do. You have the power to control your reactions to other people.

Go to the book of 2 Timothy chapter 1 verse 7:

"God did not give us a spirit that makes us afraid. He gave us a spirit of power and love and self-control." 1 Timothy 1: 7

That is one of my favorite verses! We have power over fear. You can have self – control. The older you get the more control you can have.

God has given you the ability to deal with the things of this world. You can be strong in him.

Anger Tips

It is natural to get angry or mad at others sometimes. How you deal with the anger makes a difference.

When someone gets on your nerves, makes you mad, etc., take charge over your reaction to it.

Turn to the book of James chapter 1 verses 19-20:

My dear brothers, always be willing to listen and slow to speak. Do not become angry easily. Anger will not help you live a good life as God wants. James 1: 19-20

Another one of my fave verses. When you get angry, step away and think on what you will say. Count to ten. Take a deep breath. Think if you need to get angry, say or do anything to the person who made you mad.

Remember we are living in a world where God has given everyone the ability to choose. Every choice we make has a good or bad reaction, we may not see these consequences of our choices right away. It's important to remember our choices affect many people beside ourselves.

Choose wisely in everything you do. You have the power to stop and think before you do anything! You are in charge of you!

Hopes and Dreams

Your teen years are when you start to have a plan or idea of what you want to do when you become an adult. God has given you gifts and talents to use for his purpose and to live an abundant life. What are your talents? What are some careers you can pursue with your talents? What do you love to do? Start to think about your passions. Do some research.

No other gem shines like a diamond!

Social Media Tips

Everything done through social media is there forever. Every tweet, picture, comment, post, vine, meme, etc. Please think before you post anything.

Stop. Think. Do.

Don't post naked pictures, gossip, bad words or things about you or others. You can seriously cause some major drama that will affect your life and others. Sometimes the effect can happen years later, when you try to get into college or get a job. Think of the future you.

If you have done something like this, don't be afraid or feel guilty. We all make mistakes. Confess what you did wrong to God, ask for his forgiveness, don't do it again and leave it behind you. You may try to delete the post, however there may be traces somewhere! Ask a good friend to help keep you on the right path. God is a forgiving God!

Social media can be used to have fun, but don't forget to take a break at least once a week from it. Give yourself a recharge and take part of the real world around you.

- Go to a park.

- Read books.

- Hang out with your friends.

- Volunteer.

- Exercise.

- Draw, paint, doodle...Have fun!

Take action:

- God has given you a powerful mind.
- Think of some choices you made that resulted in some good things, how about bad things?
- Write down where you see yourself in 5 years. How about 10 years?
- How do you plan to get there?
- Praise God for everything.

Space for your thoughts:

_____

_____

_____

_____

_____

I AM IN CHARGE OF ME

Dear Lord,

Thank you for all that you do, have done, and will do for this amazing young lady. You are amazing, God! I pray that her heart is open for all the love that you have for her. I pray she believes in herself and knows how much value she has to this world. I pray she loves you with all her heart, mind and soul. I pray she trusts and obeys you with her life to get all the blessings and promises you have for her. May your grace, mercy, peace and love be with her always. In Jesus' name I pray, Amen.

A SPECIAL PRAYER FOR YOU

How to pray

Praying is talking to God. Start your prayer praising God for who He is. Pray for God's will to be done. Pray some of your favorite scriptures. If you have done anything wrong, ask for forgiveness. Thank Him for forgiving you. Then you can ask for special needs for others and for you. Tell Him what is troubling you. What's on your mind. You can even sit quietly with God. End the prayer by praising and worshiping Him again!

He wants us to pray all the time! Just like you talk to your BFF's.

Praying will help you get through life. God answers prayer. Trust Him. Do what He wants you to do. The Bible is your guide!

"Always be happy. Never stop praying. Give thanks whatever happens. That is what God wants for you in Christ Jesus." 1 Thessalonians 5: 16-18

WORTH MORE THAN DIAMONDS

Pray.
Obey.
Slay.
Everyday.

GOOD NEWS

"Good news makes you feel better. Your happiness will show in your eyes." Proverbs 15: 30

How do you feel when you hear good news? Happy, excited, surprised, joyful? Yes, yes, yes and yes are my answers.

I want to share with you some good news. It's is not new news, but this news will never get old - try saying that three times!

This good, exciting news is about Jesus Christ.

Yes, I know I wrote about Him earlier in the booklet, but I want to share this fun way to explain why God sent His Son Jesus to die for us. This may help you understand more about Jesus or you can use this to tell your friends about Him.

The Good News (Gospel) in 5 precious pieces.

Gold nugget: Gold represents heaven. God is our king. Kings have bling.

Black onyx: Black onyx represents sin. Sin is when we do what God doesn't want us to do, like disrespecting our parents, being mean and gossiping.

"All people have sinned and are not good enough for God's glory." Romans 3: 23

Sin keeps us apart from God.

Red ruby: Red ruby represents the blood of Jesus who died in our place. He paid for our sins. Then three days later He rose from the grave so we can have eternal life with God.

GOOD NEWS

"God sent him to die in our place to take away our sins. We receive forgiveness through faith. And all of this is because of the blood of Jesus' death." Romans 3: 25 a-c

White pearl: We are clean and free from sin because of Jesus blood. When we admit our sins, believe in Jesus as Lord and what He did for us and ask for God's forgiveness the black onyx stain of sin gets washed away and becomes pearly white.

"If anyone belongs to Christ, then he is made new. The old things have gone; everything is made new!" 2 Corinthians 5: 18

Green jade: Jade represents spiritual growth. Reading the Bible, praying, going to a Bible based church, joining a youth group, listening and singing worship songs are some examples of how to grow in your relationship with Jesus. Quiet time talking to Jesus while walking in the park is my favorite way to connect with Him. What are some ways you like to connect with Jesus?

"Be careful. Continue strong in the faith. Have courage, and be strong. Do everything in love." 1 Corinthians 16: 13

Have hope in Jesus and you will never be hopeless!

References:

Smithsonian Institution. The Hope Diamond. https://www.si.edu/spotlight/hope-diamond. Accessed June 01, 2019.

Sons, S. The 7 Most Expensive Diamonds in the World. http://www.shzell.com/most-expensive-diamonds Accessed 1 Jun. 2019.

Winston, Harry. History and Heritage. About Harry Winston. https://www.harrywinston.com/en/history Accessed September 26, 2019

Photo credits:

Watermelon and fruits Image by Silviarita from Pixabay.

Sparrow image by Muhammad Hagnawaz from Pixabay.

Hope Diamond image by David Bjorgen.https://en.wikipedia.org/wiki/File:Hope_Diamond.jpg

REFERENCES/PHOTO CREDITS

https://creativecommons.org/licenses/by-sa/3.0/deed.en

Chapter and book cover photos by Alicia Powell of Pixistock.com.

About The Author

What if every girl knows their worth? The world will be a different place. Christina Leeman's passion is to make this known to every girl. Her two beautiful daughters and the girls in her volunteer outreach are the catalyst to this book. From the girls experiences she realizes everyone needs to believe their worth so they can live a rich life and find worth in others.

Christina Leeman is married and has two beautiful daughters. A beagle and two cats call her mom, too. Christina loves to be with her family, write, read, exercise, laugh and warm weather. She loves Jesus with all her heart, soul and mind!

Worth More Than Diamonds is her first published book.

www.ingramcontent.com/pod-product-compliance
Lightning Source LLC
Chambersburg PA
CBHW071416290426
44108CB00014B/1845